TRADITIONAL COUNTRY LIFE RECIPE S

VICTORIAN
★ ✦ ★
CHRISTMAS
★ ✦ ★
COOKERY

To Anna,
I guess now you have
all the major holidays covered.
Happy cooking!

TRADITIONAL COUNTRY LIFE RECIPE SERIES

VICTORIAN CHRISTMAS COOKERY

Bruce T. Paddock

Interior Illustrations
Alison Gail

Cover Illustration
Lisa Adams

The Brick Tower Press ™
1230 Park Avenue, New York, NY 10128
Copyright © 1994
Bruce T. Paddock
Heritage Square Museum Photos, pages 2 and 8, Copyright © Heritage Square Museum
Cooking Mold Photo, page 16, Copyright © Lydia MacLear Photography
All rights reserved under the International and Pan-American Copyright Conventions.
Printed in the United States by J. T. Colby & Company, Inc., New York.

Paddock, Bruce T.
The Traditional Country Life Recipe Series:
Victorian Christmas Cookery
Includes Index
ISBN 1-883283-06-X softcover

Library of Congress Catalog Card
Number: 94-78179
November 1994
First Edition

CONTENTS

Introduction

The Menus

The Recipes

History of the Christmas Celebration

When most Americans think of a "traditional" Christmas, they conjure up images of a dinner table covered with massive amounts of food, a fat turkey or goose right in the middle; of a Christmas tree covered with candles and brightly-colored handmade decorations; of snow drifting down outside the window beside the fireplace; of carolers in long coats and tall hats singing from door to door and then being invited in for a cup or two; of strange foods like sugar plums and figgy pudding. What most people don't realize is that this image of "Christmas as it always was" is less than a hundred and fifty years old. Every single one of those Christmas icons was an invention of the Victorian era. (Well, maybe not the snow.)

Christmas first became a huge, festive occasion in the second, third, and fourth centuries. As pagans were converted to Christianity, they converted their traditional mid-winter festival into a Christian celebration. Eventually, though, later Christians reacted against the pagan roots of the celebration. In the 1500s, Protestants reacted against the pomp, ceremony, and iconography (among other things) of the Catholics. By the time that Europeans came to this country, Christmas was a simple, somber occasion. In fact, the strict Puritans who settled New England didn't mark the holiday at all.

Things began to change in the 1800s. The Industrial Revolution had brought great prosperity to some, and had lifted many others out of poverty and into a new thing called the Middle Class. Times were good, people had money, and they wanted to celebrate. Of course, for the servants, it was another story. They spent Christmas working at their usual posts; on the day after, the employing family

The dining room of the Hale House at Heritage Square Museum decorated for a traditional Victorian Christmas, c. 1899

selected gifts (sometimes from the ones they had received and didn't want), put them into boxes, and gave them to the servants. In fact, Boxing Day is still a holiday in England and Canada.

In Victorian England, as in the United States today, cultural perceptions were created and spread by the media. One of the reasons that Christmas became so popular, and the main reason that the images and icons of a traditional Victorian Christmas have survived virtually unchanged up to today, is the writing of Charles Dickens. The John Grisham or Danielle Steele of his day, Dickens was much-loved and very widely-read. *A Christmas Carol* is only the most famous of a great number of Christmas stories—many containing ghosts—that he wrote over the years. Many, if not most, of the images that we think of as "Christmas as it always was" were to some extent the invention of, and to a large extent popularized by, one celebrated writer.

Gift Giving in Victorian Times

So, if the Victorian era saw Christmas become a time of feasting, celebrating, and gift-giving…what sort of gifts were being given? Here's one answer, or series of answers, from an 1895 magazine:

For the mistress of a home the selection offers "the embarrassment of plenty." Her five o'clock tea-table invites the most varied and dainty furnishings. One may offer a single pretty cup and saucer, or a tea-cloth with large doilies to match…. If a lady's writing-table be in evidence, be sure that she will prize any trifling addition to its furnishings. At a trifling cost one may find silver-topped mucilage-bottles, letter-clips, perpetual calendars and thermometers framed in silver… and paper-cutters.

For the young lady of the household the choice of gifts is practically unlimited…. In the manner of gifts from a young man friend, an unwritten law of conventionality limits his choices to either books, flowers or bon-bons….

An "engaged" girl, dreaming of that stray bit of paradise, her future home-nest, will be made happy by any trifle that later may find a place within it. Her pleasure in a piece of bric-à-brac or silver will anticipate the joys of wedding gifts.

The schoolgirl will rejoice in the possession of anything that seems the prerogative of her elder sister who is "out." [She] will find gratification in a pretty cardcase, a "party" fan, a bit of jewelry…a canary, if she is fond of pets….

A novelty for the small boy is a box containing modelling tools, a can of moist clay and a set of molds in the forms of animals or busts of famous men….

Among the best [gifts for men] are… cigar-cutters, dog-whistles, pocket compasses… and match-boxes engraved to imitate the autograph of the recipient.

Grandma must not be forgotten. Those who have outlived most of their contemporaries are keenly appreciative of any little attentions…. I have never seen anything so much enjoyed by an old lady as a wonder-ball. Within a ball of worsted many little gifts are wound, which reveal themselves as the yarn is unrolled in the knitting. A footstool, a musical-box, a hanging cabinet for medicines or little conveniences… a salts-bottle and a couvre-pied are things that will not fail to please.

Just a few years earlier, a different writer—presumably one with a somewhat looser grip on reality—suggested giving Mom a length of fabric, so that she could make a dress out of it. "What gift can be more acceptable to the ever-saving mother than such a dress length in a pretty soft gray, warm brown or black mixed serge, hop-sacking, Henrietta or boucette goods with all of the linings included neatly and daintily tied up?" Of course, this same writer also said, "Small boys like articles of apparel, as handkerchiefs, neckties, a suit of clothes or a new hat…," so I don't think we have to take her too seriously.

Between a young man and a young woman, Christmas gift-giving could be quite problematic. After all, "It is not good form for a young woman to give expensive gifts to any but her betrothed. Indeed, she must not give any real gift at all. If a young man has been kind to her, she may send him a card, mayhap, or a calendar of her own painting, or some little trifle, if she so desires; but it is better taste for a young woman to send nothing at all in the way of Christmas greetings to young men." Not surprisingly, the men were not let off the hook quite so easily. "A young man may give presents of books, flowers, bonbonnieres, or any pretty favors that may please his fancy, provided that he does not select jewelry, as this is not given save between those who are engaged."

"At Christmas play and have good cheer;
For Christmas comes but once a year."

Victorians managed to come up with an endless variety of ways to distribute the gifts. Presents for the servants—cash—might be hidden in the folds of a handkerchief, tucked inside a glove, or pinned to the flyleaf of a book. Sometimes each family member would be given the name of another family member to buy a gift for—very similar to the Secret Santa arrangements sometimes made in today's offices, dorms, or wherever. The gifts would be delivered to the recipients at the Christmas dinner. If a room could be spared, the gifts might be placed at one end, each tied to a long string. The strings were wound around the room, over window sills, underneath furniture, through chandeliers, and intertwined with each other. The ends were brought out the door and given to each recipient, who had to follow the string to find his or her present. But the most common spot for the gifts was hanging on the tree.

The Victorian Christmas Tree

It's hard to say just when the Christmas tree arrived in the United States, but its popularity increased greatly in the 1850s, helped by a magazine photo of Queen Victoria and Prince Albert with *their* Christmas tree. I found a short story from 1860 that describes one family's tree. It was placed on the floor in a jar of wet sand (the Christmas tree stand had evidently not been invented yet). Green baize beneath protected the floor, and green chintz above hid the unsightly jar. It seems, however, that the artist hired to illustrate the story never actually read it; his picture shows the tree sitting on a table, which was the older, English style. In the story, the tree was decorated with threaded holly berries, small bouquets of paper flowers, strings of beads, tiny flags (banners maybe?) made out of ribbons, stars and shields made from gilt paper, knots of bright ribbons, and lace bags filled with colored candies. For light, small, thin candles were wired to the branches. Each had a clear space above it to reduce the risk of fire, and Father alone lit them, and only once: just before the children dashed in to open their presents. To make sure that each one lit quickly, thereby further reducing the risk of fire, he rubbed each wick with alcohol first (do NOT try this). As noted before, the presents—even the big ones—were also hung from the tree. Only a few special ones were set aside. The importance of the gifts to the Christmas tree is underscored by a later article on decorating the house which begins, "If there are no small children in your household, you probably will forgo the Christmas tree."

Decorating the House

Leaving the tree aside, decorations for the rest of the house were both surprisingly simple and quite elaborate—simple because they consisted almost entirely of greenery and flowers; elaborate because these people were Victorians. The staple of the Christmas decorations was wreathing. Sure, wreaths were hung in the windows that faced the street. But that was just the beginning. Wreathing—thin evergreen branches attached to long lengths of wire (after all, there was no such thing as plastic garland yet)—was used to frame pictures and windows. Huge lengths of it started in the middle of the ceiling and swooped their way to the walls and down around the door frames. It started in the corners and climbed up to the ceilings, then came together and twined down the chandelier. It swagged along open sections of wall, it curtained doorways, and it filled transoms. Without wreathing, it just wouldn't have been Christmas.

To prevent the parlor from becoming a vast sea of green, flowers and berries were brought in. Of course you would expect to find poinsettias, holly, and mistletoe. But chrysanthemums were used, too, as were mountain ash berries and Christmas roses. Those who planned ahead saved the brightly-colored leaves of autumn; preserved them by pressing, drying, or dipping in wax; and used them as part of the

The top of this sideboard is decorated with wreathing for Christmas (the pheasants are permanent decorations).

Christmas decorations. Long vines like ivy or running pine were sometimes used in place of or in addition to the wreathing.

Decorating the Table

Greenery and flowers were used to decorate the dinner table, too. Evergreen branches might cover the surface between each of the guests, all leading to a multi-tiered centerpiece of flowers, moss, vines, and fruit. Or one could, "Arrange white chrysanthemums in a centrepiece with ferns. Fasten the blossoms so they will stand upright or gracefully bend, letting the ferns fill all the empty space. For a small table this will be sufficient if the ferns spread out to the ends of the table and a wreath of holly-berries edge the centre-piece. If the table be large, lay a bright red Liberty scarf loosely on it, catching down with ferns and blossoms, and fringing it with holly. Christmas roses and holly make a beautiful decoration, especially if the table be lighted with silver candelabra having little red shades. If a yellow table is preferred, the shaggy yellow chrysanthemums are most effective. Maréchal Neil roses and orchids are used in combination; gold orchids and La France roses, and white lilies and scarlet blossoms." Another source suggests much simpler table decorations: A section of white silk crumpled into graceful folds in the center of the table, twigs of holly berries tucked into the folds, and a twig of mistletoe at each place. But it goes on to suggest that a small round side table be covered with a white cloth and then entirely covered with ferns (with the stems running to the center), and in the center "a pretty basket of fruit, the handle covered with holly." Oh yes. There should also be two palms in front of the fireplace, "met with a flow of green from the mantle itself."

Setting the Table

The setting of the table was planned with the same exactitude as every other aspect of the dinner. A piece of thick flannel under the table cloth makes even the cheapest cover appear to be of much better quality. Then, "Avoid the cheap tricks of hotels and restaurants in the arrangement of napkins and table utensils. Simplicity is never ridiculous, while pretension usually is. Place the napkin on the left side of the plate with a piece of bread in its folds, the fork on the right hand, next to that the knife with the sharp edge turned from the one who is to use it." Another writer, one who avoids the restauranteur's cheap tricks but also simplicity, says, "At each place there should be placed, on the left side, an oyster-fork or a shaddock-spoon, a fork for fish, one for entrée, one for roast and one for salad. To the right should be a small silver knife for fish, a steel knife for the roast, dessert and table spoons for dessert and soup. Bread-and-butter plates are once more in fashion [1895]...." The most important rule to remember for silverware is that, as the meal progresses, the silverware should progress from the outside in.

Two items necessary to any Victorian dinner-party table, yet almost entirely forgotten today, are the menu card and the guest card. Each person's plate had another plate covering it, which was removed just before the food was served. The napkin might be placed on this cover, as might the guest card, else it would be placed just above the tip of the fork. Today, the only place we see guest cards is at weddings; one look at the guest cards reproduced on the following page and on pages 5 and 18 will tell you how far they have fallen in a hundred years. I should point out two things about these cards: First, the quotes are typeset in these examples, but I think that was done by the magazine in which I found them; I'd imagine that the hostess would write each quote by hand when she filled in each guest's name. Second, each guest got his or her own quote, preferably one appropriate to the person at that place.

Menu cards, two of which are reproduced on pages 11 and 12, were used to let the guests know what to expect. Again, the hostess would write, by hand, in as elegant a handwriting as possible, the menu for the evening. I'm not sure whether a separate menu card was put at each place,

"Frame your mind to mirth and merriment"

or if two or three or however many were placed at suitable intervals along the table. I do know that no household was complete without menu card holders, which came in a wide variety of shapes and styles. Some looked—to me, at any rate—rather like the music holders that members of a marching band use: ornate gold or brass, and with a spring so that the menu card could be clipped in.

Generally speaking, the hostess sat at one end of the table and the host opposite her at the other end. The main dish was placed in front of the host, and if there was a secondary main dish (as, for example, the cold baked ham in the menu—

For a Christmas Week Party—see page 21), it was placed at the other end, in front of the hostess. The other dishes were arranged along the sides of the table between the two; they were called "sides" or, today, "side dishes." Bowls of condiments were then strewn artistically into the remaining spaces.

I believe that then, as now, the accouterments of dinner varied widely with geographic area and socioeconomic position. The difference is that many of the elements that we today think of as being upper class—such as servants, finger bowls, and a different wine with every course, to pick just three fairly disparate examples—were much more common among the Victorian middle class. There are a number of reasons for this, one being that the gap between lower class and middle class was much wider than it is today, so a well-to-do businessman or doctor or lawyer could afford to pay the salaries of several servants. In addition, most of the members of the middle class had, as I mentioned before, joined it within recent memory, and many were desperately trying to imitate the upper class, which was their only role model. This helps explain why the late Victorian parlor was so crammed with photos, mementos, and bric-à-brac. Rich families passed things along from generation to generation, so rich people had a lot of things. So the Victorian middle class tried to acquire as many things as they could. They also served a different wine with every course, and used finger bowls; again, they were just imitating their role models.

Incidentally, finger bowls were brought out after the first course. A small folded napkin sat between the glass bowl and the plate it was brought on, to deaden the sound. A second, larger napkin was placed to the right of the

Fried Smelts, Sauce Tartare
Roast Venison, Currant Jelly
Curled Potatoes
Spinach   Creamed Mushrooms

plate. The water in the bowl was scented, usually with a lemon slice or a rose blossom. One dipped one's fingers in the water, then pressed them against the larger napkin, which was then thrown lightly over the bowl. Europeans might dip a corner of the napkin in the water and moisten their lips with it, but Americans frowned on the practice. Other sources tell me that the finger bowls were brought at the end of the meal—though whether that's instead of or in addition to at the beginning, I couldn't say. I would assume that if something particularly messy were served, the bowls would be brought out after that course.

As for wines, "the fashion changes and the modes and kinds are not the same in different States, countries, and places. However, the following are good general rules. Four wines are sufficient for an ordinary dinner, and but one, or at most two are usually served. Where three wines are served, sherry should be brought on with the soup—claret with the first course after the fish, and champagne with the roast. The general rule for serving other varieties is, that the white wines, such as sauterne and Rhine wines should be served with raw oysters, or before the soup. The soup or fish has sherry or Madeira as its accompaniment. Champagne follows with the meat, claret or red wine with the game." Don't forget that sherry should be served chilled, while claret and Madeira should be served at room temperature. The champagne can be chilled or, believe it or not, frappéd—partly frozen and served over shaved ice.

Salmon Trout, Cream Sauce

Filet of Beef with Mushrooms

Potatoes au Gratin
Green Peas   Creamed Califlower

Lemon Sherbet

Cooking in Victorian Times

As you may already have guessed, cooking itself was quite a different experience then from what it is now. The first and most obvious thing is that people cooked on coal, or sometimes even wood stoves. One (or, more likely, one's servant) would light the stove first thing in the morning, and gauge the cooking by how hot the stove was—exactly the opposite of the way we do it today.

Another interesting challenge to the Victorian cook was the lack of standardization. My favorite magazine, *Table Talk,* had a column where readers could write to the editors for cooking advice or tips; one letter from 1898 said, basically, what are these new things called "measuring cups" that I'm hearing about? A recipe might call for two teacups of sugar without really worrying about how much bigger your teacup might be than mine. Add to this instructions like "Take a lump of butter the size of an egg," and you end up with some real minefields.

Adapting Victorian Recipes

I've done my best, with the recipes in this book, to standardize them and make them easy for the modern cook to follow. If there was a conflict between taste and authenticity, I opted for taste. To give you just one example, the original instructions for cauliflower said, fairly consistently from source to source, to soak the head in water for an hour (I believe this was to soak out the bugs), and then boil it for a half an hour. The result was a soggy, waterlogged mess that tasted pretty miserable and that had to be wrapped in cheesecloth to keep it from falling apart. In this, as in many other cases, I gave directions that are more in keeping with today's tastes.

One area where I didn't adjust, though, was with the herbs. I assumed that you, like your Victorian counterpart, would be using fresh herbs. They're not hard to find; most supermarkets have plastic packets of them hanging near the produce. If I thought a fresh herb might be difficult to find, or that it wouldn't matter if you used dried herbs, I mentioned it in the recipe. If it's not mentioned, I meant fresh herbs; if you decide to use dried herbs, you'll only need one half to one third as much.

Similarly, things like cloves, nutmeg, and cinnamon are much zippier if you buy them whole, not ground. Nutmeg can be grated on an ordinary cheese grater. Cloves, cinnamon, and such can be ground up in a food processor—though I prefer to use an electric coffee mill.

Hints and Tips

I tried to keep the directions as simple as possible for this reason: I have no idea, gentle reader, who you are. You may be a gourmet chef in your own right, or you may never have prepared anything more complicated than a peanut butter and jelly sandwich. I wanted to be sure that if you were the latter, you could use this book as easily as someone who is the former. So if you have no idea what "cream the butter" or "blanch the potatoes" means, fear not; you won't find those instructions here—or, if you do, I explain them. With that in mind, though, I'm afraid that there are a couple points that I didn't get the chance to explain fully in the recipes themselves. With your permission, I'd like to spend a minute or two dealing with them here. No objections? Good.

First off, when you're roasting a chicken, duck, turkey, or goose, it's a good idea to put one of those little racks inside the roasting pan and then rest the roastee on the rack. This lets the hot air circulate underneath, which makes for more even cooking. It also makes for a much easier cleanup. One thing, though. If you're making the braised duck (the menu—*Five Courses, from soup to nuts*, see page 24), skip the rack. The ducks sit right on the vegetables.

Several recipes herein (cranberry jelly and sauce, charlotte russe, and plum pudding) call for molds. These might not be so easy to find, depending on where you live. If you're in or near an urban area, try to find a specialty gourmet shop. If you're not, I can only suggest calling places like Williams & Sonoma or Lechter's to see if they'll send one to you (I'm sorry I can't be more specific than that; I know what these places carry as I write this, but I have no idea what they'll be carrying when you read this). I have two molds that I use. One is 5 inches in diameter and 4 inches high; the other is 6 inches in diameter and 4 3/4 inches high. The large one is fine for the plum pudding, though you may have some pudding left over. I make the cranberry sauce in the smaller one, but it doesn't fill it; you'll want to get an even smaller mold or double the recipe. If you're getting a mold for the charlotte russe, don't get one like the one pictured on the next page. The spike in the middle is great for puddings, or even the cranberry sauce, but it's lousy for charlotte russe. And don't worry about how decorative your charlotte russe mold is, as the sponge cake will cover all the flutings (don't worry; you'll understand when you read the recipe). It's probably easier to use a bowl than a mold anyway.

Even the simple molds were quite elaborate 100 years ago.

There is one technique that pops up more frequently in this book than I would have guessed. It's simple to do, but a little tricky to explain, so I'd like to cover it here in depth. You'll use it whenever you make a gravy or a thick sauce, indeed, any time you try to mix a liquid into a solid (or paste). If you want to practice it, just get a can of condensed cream of mushroom soup. It comes out of the can as a thick paste, right? Then you pour in a can of water and stir. Soon you have soup. Except, if you look closely, it's not really evenly mixed. There are still bits of thick stuff floating around in the soup. Now try this. Pour just a tiny bit of liquid into the paste, then mix it in thoroughly. The result is a slightly less thick paste. Now add a tiny bit more of the liquid and mix it in thoroughly. It's still paste. Keep adding a tiny bit of liquid at a time, mixing it in thoroughly, and soon you'll have a thin paste. Then, at some cosmologically magic moment, you'll add a tiny bit of liquid, mix it in thoroughly, and the result will be a thick liquid At that point you can stir the rest of the liquid in pretty much as fast as you want. But your liquid—sauce, gravy, or cream of mushroom soup—is wonderfully smooth and homogenous.

Today, though, this is about as elaborate a mold as you are going to find.

I've done my best in this book to provide accurate step-by-step instructions that leave nothing out. Unfortunately, though, I can't provide all of the background information you might want on every subject. If you don't have a lot of experience making rolls, for example, you might want to borrow a bread-making book from the library and read the chapter (probably Chapter 1) on the basics. If you've never made a pie before, you might want to check a pie book—or even the pie section of a huge general-purpose cookbook like *Better Homes and Gardens* or *The Joy of Cooking*. And if you'd rather not mess with making your own rolls, or pickles, or whatever, don't forget—they had stores in the 1800s, too.

Using This Book

As for the book itself, its organization is rather simple. I give you actual menus from the (usually late) 1800s, then I follow them with the recipes you'll need to make the dishes from the menus. I start with a very elaborate menu, just to show you how fancy you could get if you want. I don't expect you'll want to prepare that big a feast; but if you do, many of the recipes are in the book. Then come nine menus, followed by the recipes for the items on those menus. I've thrown in a couple of extras—Yuletime favorites (of mine, anyway) that don't appear on any of the menus, but that I thought you might enjoy. One of them is the recipe for Yule dollies, like the one that appears on the cover. I close with some helpful notes and tips, direct from the Victorian sources.

As I said, I hope that everything in here is simple enough for anyone to understand. I've also tested every recipe myself, so I know that they work. If I've made a mistake—either because you don't understand what I mean by something, or because you can't get something to come out right—please don't hesitate to let me know. Write to me, care of Brick Tower Press, and I'll do what I can to ease the situation.

Acknowledgments

I'd like to thank the folks at the Heritage Square Museum Village in Los Angeles and at the Doctor's House in Glendale, California, for inspiring in me an interest in and a love for all things Victorian. I also need to thank my agent, Faith Hamlin, for making all the arrangements possible. I owe a huge debt of gratitude to my good friends Gerard Cariffe and Patty Paddock, for all of their help. Thanks, too, and much love, to my parents, Bob and Sandy Paddock, who make all things possible. My sincere thanks go to all of my friends and colleagues, too many to mention here, who provided feedback for my experiments—especially to those who were honest enough to tell me when something wasn't working. And finally, gentle reader, my thanks to you, for buying this book. I hope you enjoy it.

Bruce T. Paddock
New York City, 1994

"The guest that best becomes the table."

SAMPLE MENU
TO GIVE YOU AN IDEA OF HOW MUCH IS POSSIBLE

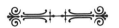

Salted Almonds

Blue Points on Half Shell
_____
Soup Crécy
_____

Olives

Boiled Red Snapper
Potatoes

Oyster Sauce
Parsley Sauce

Roasted Capon

Truffle Stuffing

Cranberry Sauce

Potato Stuffing

Roasted Goose

Apple Sauce
_____

Scalopped Tomatoes

Peas

Punch
_____

Canvas-back Duck

Baked Macaroni
_____

Currant Jelly

Tiny Lobster Cutlets, with Lettuce and French Dressing
Toasted Wafer Thins
_____

English Plum Pudding
_____

★

Coffee
_____

★

Raisins

Fruit
Sugar Plums

Nuts

A SIMPLE, BASIC MEAL

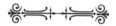

Oyster Soup

Roast Turkey with Oyster Stuffing

Baked Sweet Potatoes   *Mashed Potato*

Cauliflower   *Celery*

Cranberry Jelly

Mince Pie   *Cheese*

Fruits   *Nuts*   *Coffee*

FOR A CHRISTMAS WEEK PARTY

Chicken Croquettes
Rolls

Mayonnaise of Celery

Beef à la Mode   Baked Ham, Cold

Olives   Salted Almonds   Gherkins

Ice Cream   Coffee

★★   ★   ★★

This menu was suggested to a reader of a magazine who wrote:

I am contemplating a party for Christmas week, to be given by my daughter in honor of her brother, aged 18, and two or three who will accompany him home from school.

The editors also suggested:

Boned chicken may be substituted for the baked ham or beef à la mode, and the coffee may be served with the chicken croquettes. It would be exceedingly nice to have placed here and there around the house large punch bowls filled with lemonade. Almost any rude bowl or even a porcelain-lined preserving-kettle may be nicely covered with vines, and arranged prettily on the table and used for this purpose.

THE TRADITIONAL CHRISTMAS GOOSE

Bouillon

_____

Roast Goose   Apple Sauce

Stewed Cabbage

Mashed Potatoes   Stewed Tomatoes

_____

Mayonnaise of Celery

Cheese Fingers

_____

Mince Pie

Coffee

ADDING THE SEAFOOD COURSE

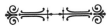

Raw Oysters in Ice Block
_____

Fried Chicken   *Cream Sauce*

Hot Milk Biscuit   *Coffee*
_____

Salad of Chicory and Halibut,   *Sauce Béarnaise*
_____

Rose Jelly   *Angel Food*

★★

You can order a block of ice from an ice dealer. Just look under "ICE" in the yellow pages.

FIVE COURSES FROM SOUP TO NUTS

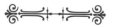

Chicken Broth with Rice

Braised Duck
Browned Turnips

Onion Stuffing
Peas

Chicken Pie

Mayonnaise of Celery

Wafers

Neufchatel

Charlotte Russe
Coffee

Fruit   Raisins   Sugar Plums   Nuts

Once you've made sugar plums—and eaten them—you will at last know what sort of visions should be dancing in your head.

SIX COURSES, BUT ONE IS JUST COFFEE

Cream of Celery Soup

———————————

Roasted Chicken   Bread Stuffing

Oyster Sauce

Browned Mashed Potatoes   Baked Macaroni

———————————

Lettuce Salad, French Dressing

Crackers   Cheese

———————————

Mince Pie   Cranberry Tart

———————————

Coffee

———————————

Raisins   Candy   Nuts

★
★   ★
★ ★

EIGHT COURSES, SOME VERY LIGHT

★
〜〜

Consommé

★
〜〜

_____

Lobster à la Newberg

_____

Roast Turkey
Peas

Cranberry Sauce
Potato Boulettes

_____

Roman Punch

_____

Macaroni Croquettes

Cream Sauce

_____

Lettuce Salad

_____

Wafers

Plum Pudding

Cheese

_____

Fruit
Coffee

FOR THOSE WHO PREFER A LESS ELABORATE MEAL

Cream of Celery Soup

—————————————

Fish à la Creme   Potato Balls

—————————————

Roasted Chicken   Cranberry Sauce

Browned Sweet Potatoes

Peas

—————————————

Lettuce Salad

French Dressing

—————————————

Wafers   Cheese

Mince Pie

Cranberry Tart

—————————————

Coffee

—————————————

Fruit   Nuts

This menu was suggested "for those who prefer a less elaborate meal and for those living away from large cities."

NINE COURSES—FOR A LARGE GATHERING

Oysters on Half Shell

★   ★

Almond Milk Soup with Rice

Salted Almonds   Celery   Olives

Halibut Baked with Fine Herbs
English Drawn Butter
Persian Potatoes

Roast Turkey   Cranberry Sauce
Rice Croquettes   Asparagus Tips
Braised Duck   Baked Macaroni

Lettuce Salad

Wafers   Brie

English Plum Pudding   Brandy Sauce

Coffee

Nuts   Fruits   Sugar Plums

CONSOMMÉ

(1) Cut the beef into 1-inch cubes and brown in a small amount of beef suet or oil.

(2) In a large pot, combine the beef, marrow bone, veal, and cold water.

(3) Cover pot and slowly bring to a boil; simmer for 3 hours.

(4) Add chicken bones, onion, turnip, carrots, and sage; simmer for another 3 hours.

(5) Remove meat bones and vegetables.

(6) Strain liquid through a colander lined with cheesecloth.

(7) Remove the fat.

(8) Clarify the liquid (see note).

NOTE: To clarify the Consommé, place Consommé in a large pot. Combine 6 teaspoons of cold water with 3 egg whites; lightly beat. Add egg mixture and 2 broken egg shells to Consommé. Bring to a boil, stirring constantly. Boil for 2 minutes then reduce heat to the lowest setting and cook for another 20 minutes. Strain liquid through a colander lined with cheesecloth.

❦ INGREDIENTS

3 pounds of beef
1 pound marrow bone
3 pounds of veal
5 quarts of cold water
bones from 1 chicken
1 onion
1 white turnip
2 carrots
1/2 cup of fresh sage

NOTE: If you have enough time between cooking and serving, the easiest way to skim off the fat is to chill the broth until the fat solidifies, then lift it off the top.

SERVES 4–6

BOUILLON

(1) Place the meat in a large pot and cover with the cold water.
(2) Cover and gently boil for 6 hours, stirring every half-hour or so.
(3) Add salt to taste.
(4) Cover the bouillon and let it cool.
(5) Remove the meat, squeezing it over the pot to get all of the liquid out.
(6) Strain the bouillon, then skim the fat off the top.
(7) Return the broth to the pot and bring it back to a boil.
(8) Season to taste with salt and pepper.

❦ INGREDIENTS

3 pounds of beef, chopped fine
3 quarts of cold water
salt
pepper

NOTE: *For this recipe, you can substitute ground beef.*

NOTE: *If you have enough time between cooking and serving, the easiest way to skim the fat is to chill the bouillon until the fat solidifies, then just lift it off the top.*

SERVES 4

CHICKEN BROTH WITH RICE

(1) Place chicken parts, carrot, onion, celery, and rice in a large pot; cover with 6 cups of cold water.
(2) Wrap bay leaf and peppercorns in a piece of cheesecloth and add to pot.
(3) Cover pot and bring to a boil.
(4) Reduce heat and simmer for half an hour.
(5) Remove the chicken, vegetables, and cheesecloth.
(6) Skim the fat off the top of the broth.
(7) Season to taste with salt and pepper.

NOTE: If you have enough time between cooking and serving, the easiest way to skim the fat is to chill the broth until the fat solidifies, then lift it off the top.

❦ INGREDIENTS

1 3–4 pound chicken, quartered
1 carrot, quartered
1 onion, quartered
1 stalk of celery, quartered
1/2 cup of uncooked rice
6 cups of cold water
1 bay leaf
4 peppercorns
cheesecloth
salt
pepper

NOTE: Don't throw the chicken out; cut the meat off the bones and use it for chicken salad, chicken croquettes, or sandwiches.

NOTE: The original recipe called for chicken, water, rice, salt, and pepper. Simple, but surprisingly tasty.

SERVES 4

OYSTER SOUP

(1) Shuck the oysters— remove the meat and reserve the liquor from each oyster.
(2) Put the liquor in a pot, add water, and bring to a boil.
(3) Cut the oysters into bite-sized pieces.
(4) When the liquor mixture is boiling, skim surface if necessary.
(5) Add the oysters, mace, salt and pepper; boil for 5 minutes.
(6) Melt butter in saucepan.
(7) Whisk in the flour.
(8) Gradually add the milk, stirring constantly.
(9) Cook without boiling until thickened.
(10) After the oysters have boiled for 5 minutes, add the milk mixture to them and stir well.
(11) Serve immediately.

NOTE: "Liquor" is the liquid inside the oyster shells.

❦ INGREDIENTS

40 whole oysters or 1 quart of oyster meat (see note)
2 cups of water
1/2 teaspoon of mace
1/2 teaspoon of salt
1/4 teaspoon of pepper
1 tablespoon of butter
1 tablespoon of flour
2 cups of milk

NOTE: Oyster meat can be bought in 1/2 pint containers. The liquor's in there, too. This is the easiest— and surprisingly, the cheapest— way to do it. If you want to buy whole oysters, you'll need about 40 to get one quart of meat.

SERVES 4–6

CREAM OF CELERY SOUP

(1) Put the celery and onion in a pot with enough water to cover.
(2) Bring to a boil, then reduce heat and simmer for 15 minutes.
(3) Drain the celery, but reserve the water.
(4) Purée the celery mixture in batches of 1 cup of celery plus 2 tablespoons of the celery water.
(5) Melt butter and whisk in flour.
(6) Gradually add milk, stirring constantly.
(7) Mix in the celery purée, salt and pepper.
(8) Heat, stirring occaisionally until well heated.
(9) Serve immediately.

❦ INGREDIENTS

1 bunch of celery, chopped
1 small onion, chopped
water
2 tablespoons of butter
2 tablespoons of flour
3 cups of milk
1 tablespoon of salt
1/2 teaspoon of pepper

NOTE: *The original recipe said to cook the celery and then pass it through a colander, but life is too short; use a blender.*

SERVES 6–8

ALMOND MILK SOUP
WITH RICE

(1) Shell the almonds. Place in a skillet and cover with boiling water. Let stand 3 minutes, then drain. Pour in cold water; rub off skins and dry on a towel.

(2) Chop the nuts in a food processor adding at least a tablespoon of chicken stock to make a paste.

(3) Scrape the paste into a large pot and gradually add the remaining stock, stirring constantly over low heat.

(4) Add milk and simmer for 30 minutes.

(5) Meanwhile, bring water to a boil.

(6) Add rice, cover, and simmer for 20 minutes.

(7) Remove the rice from heat and stir in the butter.

(8) Cover rice and let stand for 10 minutes.

(9) Spoon rice into a soup tureen and add soup.

(10) Salt to taste and serve.

❧ INGREDIENTS

1/2 pound of almonds
water for blanching the almonds (see note)
4 cups of chicken stock
2 cups of milk
2 cups of water
1 cup of rice
4 tablespoons of butter
salt

NOTE: *Step 1 describes how to "blanch" almonds.*

SERVES 8

CHEESE FINGERS

Preheat oven to 350° F.

(1) Mix together the flour, cheese, salt, baking powder, and cayenne in a bowl. Mix thoroughly with a whisk.
(2) Cut the butter into the flour mixture using a pastry blender or two knives until the mixture resembles a coarse meal.
(3) Slowly add water, mixing after each addition. If needed, add more water, 1/2 teaspoon at a time, until the dough forms a ball.
(4) Use a floured rolling pin on a lightly floured board to roll the dough out to a 1/8-inch thickness.
(5) Cut strips of dough 1/2-inch wide and place on a cookie sheet.
(6) Bake for 20-25 minutes or until golden.

❦ INGREDIENTS

1 cup of flour
1/2 cup of grated Cheddar cheese
1/4 teaspoon of salt
2 teaspoons of baking powder
1/8 teaspoon (or less) of cayenne
2 tablespoons of butter, cut into small pieces
1/3 cup of water

NOTE: I couldn't find a reference or what Cheese Fingers are supposed to look like. I just cut them into 3/4-inch strips as long as one of my fingers (3 1/2 inches).

NOTE: In the original, Step 2 called for rubbing the butter and flour between your fingers to mix them. It works, if you don't mind a little mess.

MAKES ABOUT 2 DOZEN

DINNER ROLLS

(1) Scald the milk. (Heat but don't boil it.) Add butter and set aside to cool until lukewarm.

(2) Dissolve the yeast in the water.

(3) Combine the milk, yeast, sugar, and salt in a bowl.

(4) Add enough flour to form a ball that pulls away from the sides of the bowl (some flour may not combine).

(5) Remove the dough to a lightly flowered board and let rest for 10 minutes.

(6) Knead the dough for 10 minutes, adding additional flour if necessary.

(7) Set the dough in a greased bowl; turning to grease both sides.

(8) Cover the bowl with a moist cloth and set in a warm draftless spot to rise until doubled in bulk (see note).

(9) Roll dough out to 1/4-inch thickness.

(10) Cut with a small, round cookie cutter or drinking glass.

(11) Brush the top of each disk with melted butter and stack two together.

(12) Arange stacks on a lightly greased cookie sheet and brush the sides with melted butter to facilitate easy separation after the rolls are baked.

(13) Cover and let rise again.

Preheat oven to 400° F.

(14) Bake for 15 minutes or until golden.

NOTE: The water for the yeast should feel warm but not hot on your wrist.

NOTE: To test if dough is fully risen, press a finger into the dough. If the dent remains, the dough is just right.

NOTE: Serve with butter and several kinds of jams or jellies on the table, too.

❦ INGREDIENTS

2 cups of milk
1/2 cup of butter, melted
2 1/4-ounce packets of dried yeast
1/2 cup of lukewarm water
2 tablespoons of sugar
1/2 teaspoon of salt
6 cups of flour, divided
1/2 cup of butter
1 teaspoon of salt

NOTE: To knead dough, push it down and away from you with both hands. Turn it one quarter-turn and fold the top half up and back toward you. Then push it all down and away from you. Do this for 10 minutes—set a timer so you don't loose track of time.

MAKES 10–20 ROLLS

SALAD OF
CHICORY AND HALIBUT

Preheat oven to 400° F.

(1) Combine the flour, salt and pepper.
(2) Dredge the fish in the flour mixture, and place in a shallow lightly greased baking dish. Dot with butter.
(3) Bake for 15 minutes or until the fish flakes when separated with a fork.
(4) Remove from oven and transfer to a dish. Cover and chill fish for 1 hour.
(5) Tear the chicory into bit-size pieces.
(6) Cut the cold fish into small bite-size pieces.
(7) Place the chicory and fish into a salad bowl and toss to blend.
(8) Serve with Sauce Béarnaise.

❧ INGREDIENTS

1 pound halibut steak
2 cups of flour
1/4 teaspoon of salt
1/4 teaspoon of pepper
2 tablespoons of butter
1 head of chicory
Sauce Béarnaise (see next page)

SERVES 4–6

SAUCE BÉARNAISE

(1) Mix the vinegar, salt, nutmeg, shallots, chervil, and tarragon in a saucepan. Heat, stirring often, until reduced to 1 tablespoon; strain.

(2) Put the egg yolks in the top of a double boiler over gently boiling water. Beat with a whisk until they are smooth.

(3) Add the vinegar mixture to the egg yolks.

(4) Add the butter in a steady stream, stirring constantly.

(5) Add the lemon juice, stirring constantly.

(6) Add some finely chopped chervil, tarragon, and parsley.

(7) Serve on the side, or over the salad.

NOTE: *This is just barely enough sauce to cover the previous salad. It's so good, you may want to double the recipe, then find other ways to use the left-over sauce.*

❦ INGREDIENTS

2 tablespoons of vinegar
1/8 teaspoon of salt
1/4 of a nutmeg, grated
1 tablespoon of chopped shallots
1 tablespoon of chopped chervil
1 tablespoon of chopped tarragon
4 egg yolks
1/2 pound of butter, melted
juice of 1 lemon
chervil
tarragon
parsley

NOTE: *Fresh chervil can be hard to find. If you use dried chervil, only use half as much (or maybe even a little less).*

LETTUCE SALAD
WITH FRENCH DRESSING

(1) Pick over and wash the lettuce.

(2) Thoroughly dry each lettuce leaf.

(3) Tear each leaf into bite size pieces.

(4) Place the lettuce in a glass dish or bowl.

(5) Garnish with radishes, onion, cucumber, and egg.

(6) Combine the salt and vinegar or lemon juice; let stand for 5 minutes to dissolve the salt.

(7) Add the pepper.

(8) Gradually add the oil, stirring constantly.

(9) Just before serving, whip the dressing with a whisk.

(10) Pour over the salad.

(11) Serve immediately.

NOTE: *In my 1875 cookbook the author suggests making a salad as follows: "…break the leaves apart one by one from the stalk and throw them into a pan of cold water; rinse them well, lay them into a salad bowl or a deep dish, lay the largest leaves first, put the next size upon them, then lay on the finest white leaves; cut*

❦ INGREDIENTS

1 head of lettuce
4 small radishes, thinly sliced
1 small red onion, thinly sliced
1 small cucumber, thinly sliced
2 hard boiled eggs, sliced

1 teaspoon of salt
2 tablespoons of cider vinegar or lemon juice
1/2 teaspoon of white pepper
3/4 cup of olive oil

hard boiled eggs in slices or quarters and lay them at equal distances around the edge and over the salad…. Or, having picked and washed the lettuce, cut the leaves small; put the cut salad in a glass dish or bowl, pour a salad dressing over and serve; or, garnish with small red radishes, cut in halves or slices; pour a salad dressing over when ready to serve."

SERVES 4

LOBSTER À LA NEWBURG

(1) Boil the lobster for 10–15 minutes in enough water to cover.
(2) Split the shells and remove the meat; cut into small pieces.
(3) Melt 6 tablespoons of butter in a pan.
(4) Add the lobster meat, sugar, salt, and cayenne pepper.
(5) Cook over high heat for 2–3 minutes.
(6) Gradually whisk in the sherry and cook until half the liquid in the pan boils away.
(7) Add 2 cups of cream in a steady stream, stirring constantly. Cook until half the liquid in the pan boils away.
(8) Mix the egg yolks with the remaining cup of cream, then add to the pan.
(9) Add 4 tablespoons of butter.
(10) Cook over low heat without boiling until thickened.
(11) Serve over a bed of rice.

❦ INGREDIENTS

3 1 1/2-pound lobsters
10 tablespoons of butter, divided
a pinch of powdered sugar
pinch of salt
pinch of cayenne pepper
2 cups of sherry
3 cups of cream, divided
6 egg yolks

NOTE: If you don't wish to cook the lobster yourself, many places that sell lobster will steam them for you—often at no charge.

SERVES 3–4

FISH À LA CREME

Preheat oven to 350° F.

(1) Melt butter in a saucepan.
(2) Add onion and sauté until transparent.
(3) Combine the flour, mace, and parsley.
(4) Add flour mixture to the butter and whisk until smooth.
(5) Gradually add the milk, stirring until well blended after each addition.
(6) Add bay leaf.
(7) Simmer until thickened; stirring constantly.
(8) Lightly beat the egg yolks and add to the sauce.
(9) Strain and season to taste with salt and pepper.
(10) Pour a layer of sauce into a 6x6-inch baking dish. Cover the sauce layer with a layer of fish, then another layer of sauce, etc. Finish with a layer of sauce.
(11) Sprinkle the bread crumbs on top and dot with butter.
(12) Bake for 40 minutes or until golden brown.

❧ INGREDIENTS

1 tablespoon of butter
1/2 a small onion
2 tablespoons of flour
1/4 teaspoon of mace
1/4 teaspoon of parsley
2 cups of milk
1 bay leaf
2 egg yolks
salt
pepper
4 tablespoons of bread crumbs
butter
4 cups of cold, cooked fish, boned

SERVES 4

BEEF À LA MODE

Preheat oven to 325° F.

(1) Grind up the cloves and the allspice berries and place in a small bowl.
(2) Add the mace, savory, parsley, thyme, and marjoram.
(3) Cut the bacon into 1/4-inch slices. You should get 4 or 5.
(4) Trim each slice so that it is as long as the roast is wide.
(5) Dredge each slice in the seasonings, then cut a slit in the roast and place the bacon slice inside, spacing them evenly along the roast.
(6) Dredge the roast in flour and brown in a heavy-bottomed pot or Dutch oven to sear in the juice; then set the beef in a roasting pan.
(7) Add the water to the pan.
(8) Cook for 1 1/2 hours.
(9) Remove roast from the oven and let rest for 20 minutes before carving it.
(10) Scrape the bottom of the roasting pan to incorporate all the tasty pan juices. Strain the gravy and serve it on the side.

❦ INGREDIENTS

20 cloves
1/2 teaspoon of allspice berries
1/2 teaspoon of mace
1/2 teaspoon of dried savory
2 teaspoons of parsley, chopped fine
1 teaspoon of thyme, chopped fine
1 teaspoon of marjoram, chopped fine
1/4 pound of unsliced bacon
3–4 pound beef roast or chuck round or brisket
2 cups of water

NOTE: *If fresh herbs are unavailable substitute dried herbs. Use 1 teaspoon of parsley and 1/2 teaspoon each of thyme and marjoram. Talk with your butcher about how large a roast you'll need. A 3-pound roast should serve four people well.*

SERVES 4–6

BAKED HAM

Preheat oven to 350° F.

(1) Slash the fat on the ham with a knife and place in a roasting pan.

(2) Mix the flour and water into a paste and spread it over the cut surface of the ham.

(3) Pour the cider into the pan.

(4) Bake the ham for 20 minutes per pound, basting every 15 minutes.

(5) About 20 minutes before the ham is done, remove it from the oven, scrape off the paste and cut off the rind.

(6) Increase the oven temperature to 450° F.

(7) Meanwhile, turn the ham rind-side up and brush it with the beaten egg.

(8) Dust the ham with bread crumbs.

(9) Return the ham to the oven and bake until the crumbs are golden brown.

To Make the Sauce:

(10) Melt the butter, then mix in the flour to make a roux. Cook until it is lightly browned.

(11) Combine the alcohol and cooking juices; slowly add it to the roux. Stir and cook over a low heat until it's smooth and creamy.

(12) Season to taste with nutmeg, salt, and cayenne.

(13) Serve ham with sauce on the side.

NOTE: *The smallest whole ham you'll find will be 12 or 13 pounds, which will serve 10-15 people. A 5 pound ham is part of a ham, which your butcher will cut off for you.*

NOTE: *The rind is the reddish shell-like material that covers the whole ham (except, of course, the cut surface of your piece).*

❦ INGREDIENTS

1 5 pound ham (see note)
6 tablespoons of flour
6 tablespoons of water
1 quart of cider
1 egg, beaten
bread crumbs

Sauce:
2 tablespoons of butter
2 tablespoons of flour
1 cup of champagne or port or fresh
    cider
1 cup of reserved cooking juices
2 nutmegs, grated
salt
cayenne

SERVES 6–8

ROAST GOOSE

Preheat oven to 450° F.

(1) Remove the innards from the goose.

(2) Rinse the goose thoroughly, inside and out.

(3) Combine the onions, bread crumbs, mashed potatoes, butter, egg yolks, and sage.

(4) Pack the stuffing loosely into the goose, stuffing both neck and body cavities; prick the skin all over.

(5) Place the goose on a rack in a shallow roasting pan.

(6) Adjust the oven racks so that the goose sits in the middle of the oven.

(7) Roast for 1 hour.

(8) Pour off the fat every 20 minutes.

(9) Reduce heat to 325° F. and cook for 2-2 1/2 hours more.

(10) Simmer the neck and giblets in 4 cups of water for 1 1/2 hours.

(11) Set the cooked goose on a plate for 20 minutes or so before you carve it.

(12) Pour off all but 2 tablespoons of fat from the drippings.

(13) Place the roasting pan on a burner (or two), and scrape the bottom to incorporate the tasty browned bits.

(14) Whisk in enough flour to make a thick paste.

(15) Slowly stir in enough giblet cooking liquid or chicken stock to make a thin gravy.

(16) Continue to simmer until the gravy has thickened.

(17) Season to taste with salt and pepper.

NOTE: Your butcher will tell you what size goose to buy. As an example, a 12-pounder (the smallest you're likely to find) should feed 4 people. This should be enough stuffing for a small to medium-sized goose. If you have too much, put the extra in a baking dish, cover with foil, and bake next to the goose for 45 minutes.

❦ INGREDIENTS

1 10–12 pound goose
2 cups of chopped onions
2 cups of day old bread crumbs
2 cups of Mashed Potatoes (see page 63)
2 tablespoons of melted butter
3 egg yolks
8 tablespoons of sage, chopped fine
flour
giblet cooking liquid or chicken stock
salt
pepper

SERVES 4

BRAISED DUCK

Preheat oven to 350° F.

(1) Put the onion, carrot, turnip, and celery in a large roasting pan.
(2) Set the ducks on top of the vegetables, then pour in the stock.
(3) Cover and cook until tender, approximately 1 hour.
(4) Remove the ducks and reserve the liquid.
(5) In a saucepan, heat the butter until it's very brown.
(6) Add the flour and whisk until smooth. Cook until brown.
(7) Gradually whisk in 2 cups of the reserved cooking juices (be sure to remove the fat that has risen to the top).
(8) Add the mushrooms, port, salt and pepper.
(9) Bring the gravy to a boil, then reduce the heat and simmer until thickened.

❦ INGREDIENTS

1 onion, sliced
1 carrot, sliced
1 white turnip, sliced
3 stalks of celery, sliced
2 ducks (about 5 pounds each, dressed and cleaned)
1 quart of chicken or vegetable stock
2 tablespoons of butter
2 tablespoons of flour
2 medium mushrooms, chopped fine
2 tablespoons of port
salt and pepper to taste

NOTE: If you need to serve more than 6, put as many ducks in the roasting pan as will fit. If you need to use a second roasting pan, follow this procedure for each one and increase the amount of sauce accordingly.

SERVES 5-6

ROAST TURKEY

(1) Remove the innards from the turkey.
(2) Rinse the turkey thoroughly, inside and out.
(3) Rub salt into the turkey, inside and out.
(4) Pack the stuffing loosely into the turkey, stuffing both neck and the body cavities.
(5) Place the turkey on a rack in a roasting pan.
(6) Adjust the racks so that the turkey sits in the middle of the oven.
(7) Bake for 25 minutes a pound, basting with melted butter every 15 minutes.
(8) If you want to use the giblets in the gravy, cover all but the liver with cold water and bring to a boil. Reduce heat and simmer for 40 minutes. Add the liver and simmer for 5 more minutes. When done, chop them fine.
(9) Set the cooked turkey on a plate for 20 minutes or so before you carve it.
(10) Pour off all but about a half a cup of the fat from the drippings.

INGREDIENTS

1 10 pound turkey
salt
stuffing (starts on page 55)
8 tablespoons of butter, melted
flour
giblet cooking liquid or milk
salt
pepper

(11) Place the roasting pan on a burner (or two), and scrape the bottom to incorporate the tasty browned bits.
(12) Stir in enough flour to turn it into a thick paste.
(13) Slowly stir in enough giblet cooking liquid or milk to make a thin gravy. Add the giblets.
(14) Continue to simmer until the gravy has thickened.
(15) Season to taste with salt and pepper.

SERVES 6–8

ROASTED CHICKEN

(1) Remove the innards from the chicken.

(2) Rinse the chicken thoroughly, inside and out.

(3) Season with salt and pepper, inside and out.

(4) Pack the stuffing loosely into the chicken, stuffing both neck and the body cavities.

(5) Place the chicken on a rack in a roasting pan.

(6) Adjust the oven racks so the chicken sits in the middle of the oven.

(7) Bake for 25 minutes a pound, basting with melted butter every 15 minutes.

(8) If you want to use the giblets in the gravy, place all but the liver in a saucepan and cover with cold water; bring to a boil. Reduce heat and simmer for 40 minutes. Add the liver and simmer for 5 more minutes. When done, chop them fine.

(9) Set the cooked chicken on a plate.

(10) Pour off all but about a half a cup of the fat from the drippings.

❦ INGREDIENTS

1 3–5 pound chicken
salt
flour
giblet cooking liquid or milk
salt
pepper

(11) Place the roasting pan on a burner (or two), and scrape the bottom to incorporate the tasty browned bits.

(12) Whisk in enough flour to turn it into a thick paste.

(13) Slowly stir in enough giblet cooking liquid or milk to make a thin gravy. Add the giblets.

(14) Simmer until the gravy has thickened.

(15) Season to taste with salt and pepper.

SERVES 6–8

FRIED CHICKEN
WITH CREAM SAUCE

(1) Separate the chicken wings, legs, thighs, and breast halves. Save the back and wing tips for stock or soup.
(2) Mix together the flour, tarragon, salt and pepper in a bowl.
(3) Dip each piece of chicken in butter, then dredge in the flour mixture until it's thickly covered with flour.
(4) Heat oil in a frying pan until it is very hot but not smoking.
(5) Cook the chicken for 10–15 minutes per side.
(6) Set the chicken to drain, and pour out all but about 1 tablespoon of fat.
(7) Whisk in the flour to form a smooth paste, scraping the bottom to incorporate the tasty browned bits.
(8) Add the cream slowly, mixing until it becomes a smooth sauce.
(9) Season with salt and pepper to taste.

❦ INGREDIENTS

1 3–4 pound frying chicken
1 cup of flour
8 tablespoons of dried tarragon
1 teaspoon of salt
1/2 teaspoon of pepper
6 tablespoons of butter, melted
1–2 cups of cooking oil
1 tablespoon of flour
1 cup of cream
salt
pepper

NOTE: *If you heat the oil to 350° F., almost none of it will soak into the meat.*

SERVES 4

51

CHICKEN CROQUETTES

(1) Place chicken in a large pot and cover with boiling water; simmer for 1/2 hour.
(2) Cut the meat off the bones and set aside to cool.
(3) Scald the milk. (Heat but don't boil it.)
(4) Melt the butter in a saucepan.
(5) Whisk in the flour.
(6) Add the milk very slowly to the flour mixture, whisking until smooth.
(7) Simmer, stirring constantly, until thickened.
(8) Cut the chicken into small cubes.
(9) Thoroughly mix the 4 cups of chicken, sauce, salt, onion powder, cayenne, and nutmeg.
(10) Chill overnight.
(11) Form chicken into conical or pear shaped croquettes.
(12) Dip each croquette into the egg, and turn to evenly coat.
(13) Roll each croquette in bread crumbs.
(14) Heat the cooking oil in a deep, heavy pan (see note).
(15) Immerse the croquettes in the oil and cook until they are golden brown; about 1–2 minutes.

❦ INGREDIENTS

1 5-pound chicken, quartered
4 cups of milk
2 tablespoons of butter
3–4 heaping tablespoons of flour
2 teaspoons of salt
1/4 teaspoon of onion powder
1/8 teaspoon of cayenne
1/2 a nutmeg, grated
1 egg, beaten
2 cups of bread crumbs
3–4 cups of cooking oil

NOTE: *Test oil by tearing off a small piece of bread and dropping it into the oil. If nothing happens, the oil is not hot enough. If the bread turns brown, it's perfect. If the bread burns or turns black, the oil is too hot—the croquette will cook before it can heat through.*

MAKES 8–10 CROQUETTES

CHICKEN PIE

Preheat oven to 450° F.

(1) Peel and cut potatoes into small cubes.
(2) Place potatoes into a medium sized saucepan and cover with boiling water.
(3) Boil for 15 minutes; drain.
(4) Thinly slice the carrots and place in a saucepan.
(5) Cover carrots with boiling water and boil for 8 minutes.
(6) In a large bowl, combine chicken, ham, potatoes, and carrots.
(7) Melt butter in a saucepan.
(8) Add onion and cook until transparent.
(9) Combine onions with the gravy.
(10) Roll half of the dough out to fit a 12-inch pie plate with 1/2-inch overlap.
(11) Place the lower crust into the pie plate and trim the edges.
(12) Place half of the chicken mixture into the pie plate and cover with half of the gravy; repeat.
(13) Roll out the remaining dough.
(14) Moisten the edge of the lower crust with water.

❋ INGREDIENTS

3 medium potatoes
2 carrots
4 cups of cooked, leftover chicken, cubed
1/2 pound of cooked ham, cubed
2 tablespoons of butter, melted
1 small onion, sliced
2 cups of leftover gravy
Old-Fashioned Pie Pastry (see page 86)

(15) Cover the pie with the upper crust; trim and crimp the edges together.
(16) Use a fork to poke a few holes in the crust.
(17) Bake for 25-30 minutes or until the crust is golden brown.

MAKES 1 12-INCH PIE

BAKED MACARONI

Preheat oven to 350° F.

(1) Place a layer of macaroni in a 3-quart baking dish.
(2) Top with a layer of cheese.
(3) Season with salt and pepper.
(4) Repeat the layers until all ingredients are used up, finishing with a layer of macaroni.
(5) Cut the butter into small bits and strew over the top.
(6) Pour the cream over the top.
(7) Bake until golden brown—about 20 minutes.

NOTE: I have followed the Victorian custom of using the word "macaroni" to refer to any type of pasta. "In this country, it is a sort of a luxury among the upper classes; but there is no good reason, considering its price, why it should not enter more extensively into the food of our working classes....Spighetti (sic)

❦ INGREDIENTS

1 pound of macaroni, cooked
1/2 pound of Cheddar cheese, grated
salt
pepper
2 tablespoons of butter
1 /2 cup of heavy cream

is the most delicate form of macaroni that comes to this country." Nonetheless, I'd recommend fettucini for this dish.

NOTE: For variety, substitute Parmesan or Romano, or a combination of the two, for the Cheddar.

SERVES 6–8

OYSTER STUFFING

(1) Crumble the bread to make about 4 cups of bread crumbs.
(2) Chop the oysters into small pieces.
(3) Melt the butter.
(4) Stir the oysters, butter, thyme, salt and pepper into the bread crumbs.

❧ INGREDIENTS

14 slices of day-old bread
10 oysters (1 cup of meat)
1/2 pound of butter
2 teaspoons of thyme
1/4 teaspoon of salt
1/4 teaspoon of pepper

MAKES ENOUGH TO STUFF
A 15-POUND TURKEY

BREAD STUFFING

(1) Crumble the bread into bread crumbs.
(2) Melt the butter in a large pot.
(3) Add in the onion and sauté until the onion is translucent.
(4) Combine the bread crumbs, parsley, salt and pepper.
(5) Stir butter and onion into bread crumb mixture.

❧ INGREDIENTS

8 slices of day-old bread
1/4 pound of butter
1/4 cup of chopped onion
2 teaspoons of parsley
salt and pepper to taste

MAKES ENOUGH TO STUFF
A 7-POUND CHICKEN

ONION STUFFING

(1) Bring the water to a boil.
(2) Add the butter, celery, and onion to the boiling water and simmer for 5 minutes.
(3) Add the poultry seasoning, parsley, mustard, bread crumbs, salt, and pepper; mix well with a fork.
(4) Place the stuffing in a covered baking dish in the oven with the main dish during the last half hour of roasting.

❦ INGREDIENTS

1 1/2 cups of water
1/2 cup of butter
1/2 cup of diced celery
1 1/2 cups of minced onion
1 teaspoon of poultry seasoning (optional)
1/2 cup of minced parsley
2 teaspoons of dry mustard
12 cups of lightly-packed day-old bread crumbs
salt and pepper to taste

MAKES ENOUGH TO STUFF
A 15-POUND TURKEY

CRANBERRY JELLY

(1) Put the berries into the boiling water. Boil rapidly for 5 minutes.
(2) Pour the mixture into a jelly bag and suspend above a large bowl for 24 hours.
(3) Return the strained liquid to the pot.
(4) Stir in sugar and bring to a boil.
(5) Pour the liquid into a greased mold or bowl.
(6) Chill for several hours.
(7) Turn out onto a plate and serve.

NOTE: If you use a wooden or bamboo utensil, it will end up bright red. You can clean it by soaking it in boiling water for a couple of minutes.

❦ INGREDIENTS

1 pound of cranberries
2 cups of boiling water
1 cup of sugar

NOTE: This is half the sugar called for in the original recipe, and the jelly is still very sweet (I assume that cranberries were more tart a hundred years ago). You may want to use 1/2–3/4 of a cup of sugar.

SERVES 6

CRANBERRY SAUCE

(1) Place the berries into the boiling water; cook until berries begin to pop.
(2) Stir in the sugar and bring to a boil.
(3) Pour the mixture into a mold or bowl.
(4) Chill for several hours.
(5) Turn out onto a plate and serve.

NOTE: If you use a wooden or bamboo utensil, it will end up bright red. You can clean it by soaking it in boiling water for a couple of minutes.

❦ INGREDIENTS

1 pound of cranberries
2 cups of boiling water
1 cup of sugar

NOTE: This is half the sugar called for in the original recipe, and the jelly is still very sweet (I assume that cranberries were more tart a hundred years ago). You may want to use 1/2–3/4 of a cup of sugar.

SERVES 6

APPLESAUCE

(1) Core, quarter, and chunk the apples.
(2) Place the apples in a pot, and add the water.
(3) Bring to a boil, then simmer for 10 minutes, stirring constantly.
(4) Pass the apples (and whatever's left of the water) through a sieve, strainer, or food processor.
(5) Return the applesauce to the heat.
(6) Add the butter and stir until melted.
(7) Add the sugar and nutmeg to taste.

NOTE: The seasonings will vary according to your tastes and the taste of the apples you use. I usually start with 2 tablespoons of sugar and 1/4 of a nutmeg, grated.

INGREDIENTS

6 apples
1/2 cup of water
2 tablespoons of butter
nutmeg
sugar

SERVES 4

ENGLISH DRAWN BUTTER

(1) Melt the butter in a small saucepan.
(2) Whisk in salt and flour to form a smooth paste.
(3) Gradually add the stock, stirring constantly.
(4) Add lemon juice.
(5) Season to taste with salt and pepper.
(6) Serve with fish.

❧ INGREDIENTS

8 tablespoons of butter
1/8 teaspoon of salt
1 heaping teaspoon of flour
1 cup of warm fish stock or water
1/2 teaspoon of lemon juice

SERVES 4

HOMEMADE MAYONNAISE

(1) Combine the egg yolks, mustard, lemon juice, salt, and pepper in the bowl of a food processor and process for 1 minute.

(2) With the motor running, add the oil in a very fine stream. After half the oil is mixed in, you can begin to pour a little faster.

NOTE: *If you pour the oil too quickly, the mayonnaise will separate. This doesn't have to be a problem. Just beat another egg yolk in another bowl, and then mix in the separated first try. Just do it more slowly this time. Then continue adding the rest of the oil.*

✿ INGREDIENTS

2 egg yolks
1/4 teaspoon of mustard powder
1 tablespoon of lemon juice
a pinch of salt
a pinch of cayenne
1 cup of olive oil

OYSTER SAUCE

(1) Heat the oysters in their liquor for 3 minutes over low heat.
(2) Melt the butter in a saucepan.
(3) Add flour and whisk until smooth.
(4) Add a small amount of milk to the flour mixture and whisk until it forms a smooth paste.
(5) Slowly whisk in the remaining milk.
(6) Add oyster mixture to the sauce.
(7) Season with salt and pepper.

NOTE: *"Liquor" is the liquid inside the oyster shells.*

❦ INGREDIENTS

2 cups of milk
1 tablespoon of flour
1/4 pound of butter
1 cup of shucked oysters, reserve liquor
1/2 teaspoon of salt
1/2 teaspoon of pepper

NOTE: *Oyster meat can be bought in 1/2 pint containers. The liquor's in there, too. This is the easiest— and surprisingly, the cheapest— way to do it. If you want to buy whole oysters, you'll need about 10 to get one cup of meat.*

MASHED POTATOES

(1) Rinse, peel, and cut the potatoes into thirds.
(2) Cover potatoes with boiling water, and cook for 15 minutes.
(3) Pass the potatoes through a ricer and return to pot.
(4) Add the cream, butter, and salt.
(5) Beat with a fork until they're light, fluffy, and very thick.

NOTE: *A ricer is a tool that looks kind of like a huge garlic press. It easily makes smooth, lump-free mashed potatoes.*

☙ INGREDIENTS

8 medium-sized baking or russet potatoes
2 cups of heavy cream
4 tablespoons of butter
salt to taste

SERVES 6–8

63

PERSIAN POTATOES

(1) Melt the butter in a pan.
(2) Add the onion and sauté for 2 minutes.
(3) Add the potatoes and stock.
(4) Simmer gently until the potatoes are tender when pierced with a fork, approximately 10–20 minutes.
(5) Place potatoes in a serving bowl and sprinkle the parsley on top.
(6) Season to taste with salt and pepper.

✿ INGREDIENTS

2 tablespoons of butter
1 medium onion, chopped fine
5 medium-sized baking or russet potatoes, diced
1 cup of chicken stock
1 tablespoon of chopped fresh parsley
salt and pepper to taste

SERVES 4

BROWNED MASHED POTATOES

Preheat oven to 400° F.

(1) Rinse, peel, and cut the potatoes into thirds.
(2) Cover potatoes with boiling water, and cook for 15 minutes.
(3) Pass the potatoes through a ricer and return to pot.
(4) Add the cream, butter, and salt.
(5) Beat with a fork until they're light and fluffy.
(6) Place the potatoes into a buttered baking dish.
(7) Score all over with a knife.
(8) Sprinkle with coarse bread crumbs.
(9) Pour melted butter over the top.
(10) Bake until golden brown.

NOTE: A ricer is a tool that looks kind of like a huge garlic press. It easily makes smooth, lump-free mashed potatoes.

❦ INGREDIENTS

8 medium-sized baking or russet potatoes
2 cup of heavy cream
4 tablespoons of butter
salt to taste
6 tablespoons of bread crumbs
4 tablespoons of butter, melted

SERVES 6–8

POTATO BOULETTES

(1) Combine potatoes, cream, 2 egg yolks, onion powder, salt, marjoram, thyme, and parsley in a large saucepan.

(2) Cook over a medium heat, stirring constantly, until mixture pulls away from the sides of the saucepan; chill.

(3) Shape mixture into little round boulettes approximately 2–3 inches in diameter.

(4) Dip each one in the remaining eggs, then roll each one in the bread crumbs.

(5) Heat the oil and deep-fry the boulettes until they are golden-brown, approximately 1 to 2 minutes.

(6) Remove boulettes from oil and drain on paper towels.

(7) Keep warm in a 350° F. oven until ready to serve.

❦ INGREDIENTS

2 cups of Mashed Potatoes (see page 63)
4 tablespoons of cream
2 egg yolks, beaten
1 teaspoon of onion powder
1 teaspoon of salt
1/2 teaspoon of dried marjoram
1/2 teaspoon of thyme
1 tablespoon of parsley, chopped
2 eggs, beaten
bread crumbs
vegetable oil

NOTE: *Test the hot oil by tearing off a small piece of bread and dropping it in. If nothing happens, the oil is not hot enough. If the bread turns brown, it's perfect. If the bread burns or turns black, the oil is too hot—the boulette will cook before it can heat through.*

MAKES 8–10 BOULETTES

BAKED SWEET POTATOES

Preheat oven to 375° F.

(1) Rinse the sweet potatoes thoroughly.
(2) Bake them for about 45 minutes
(3) The sweet potatoes are done when a fork slides in easily once it gets past the skin.

❦ INGREDIENTS

6–8 sweet potatoes

SERVES 6-8

BROWNED
SWEET POTATOES

Preheat oven to 350° F.

(1) Remove potato skins.
(2) Mash sweet potatoes with a potato masher.
(3) Add the butter and salt.
(4) Place the sweet potatoes into a buttered baking dish.
(5) Bake until golden brown.

❦ INGREDIENTS

6 sweet potatoes, baked
6 tablespoons of butter
salt to taste

SERVES 6

ASPARAGUS TIPS
ON TOAST POINTS

(1) Cut the tips off the asparagus.

(2) Steam tips for 10 minutes or until they are bright green.

(3) Meanwhile, cut off the crusts of each slice of bread.

(4) Toast, butter, and cut the bread into quarters.

(5) Remove the asparagus from the steamer, reserving the cooking liquid for later.

(6) Arrange asparagus tips prettily on the toast.

(7) Melt the butter in a saucepan.

(8) Add the flour and whisk until smooth.

(9) Gradually add cream and then 1/4 cup of reserved cooking water, stirring constantly.

(10) Slowly bring to a boil, then reduce heat and cook until thickened.

(11) Season to taste with salt and pepper.

(12) Pour the sauce over the asparagus.

❦ INGREDIENTS

1 bunch of asparagus
4 slices of bread
butter
1 tablespoon of butter
1 tablespoon of flour
1/4 cup of cream
salt
pepper

SERVES 4

CAULIFLOWER

(1) Cut the stem close to the flowerets. Cut it evenly, so that the head can sit solidly on this base.

(2) Place the cauliflower in a steamer over boiling water.

(3) Steam the cauliflower for 20-30 minutes.

(4) While the cauliflower is steaming, melt the butter in a pan.

(5) Add the flour and whisk until smooth.

(6) Slowly add in the milk or cream, whisking after each addition until smooth.

(7) Add the salt and pepper, and simmer, stirring constantly, until sauce has thickened.

(8) Place the cauliflower in a shallow serving dish, and pour the sauce over the top.

(9) Serve immediately.

❦ INGREDIENTS

1 head of cauliflower
2 tablespoons of butter
2 tablespoons of flour
1 cup of milk or cream
1/2 teaspoon of salt
1/4 teaspoon of pepper

NOTE: You might want to add some finely chopped parsley to the sauce just before you pour it. English Drawn Butter (see page 60) made with chicken stock is also a good substitute for the cream sauce.

SERVES 6

STEWED TOMATOES

(1) To peel, plunge each tomato into boiling water for 30 seconds, place in cold water to cool, then peel off the skin.
(2) Cut tomatoes into small chunks.
(3) Combine the tomatoes in a pot with one or two slices of onion.
(4) Cover pot, and cook over a low heat for half an hour.
(5) Add the butter, sugar, and bread crumbs.
(6) Season to taste with salt and pepper.

NOTE: The amount of bread crumbs you use may vary with your tastes and the juiciness of your tomatoes.

❧ INGREDIENTS

6 medium-sized tomatoes
1 small onion, sliced
1 tablespoon of butter
1 teaspoon of sugar
1/2 cup of bread crumbs
salt
pepper

SERVES 4–6

STEWED CABBAGE

(1) Remove the white core, wash, and slice the cabbage.
(2) Melt butter in a large pot.
(3) Add the onions and cook until transparent.
(4) Add cabbage, apple, sugar, vinegar, and nutmeg.
(5) Stir and cook over a low heat until tender—about 15 minutes.
(6) Season to taste with salt and pepper.
(7) Serve.

❧ INGREDIENTS

1 small red cabbage
4 tablespoons of butter
1 small onion, finely chopped
1 tart apple, cubed
1 tablespoon of sugar
1 tablespoon of vinegar
a pinch of nutmeg
salt and pepper

NOTE: The original recipe simply called for cabbage, butter, salt, pepper, and vinegar. Simple, but tasty if you would care to try it.

SERVES 4

BROWNED TURNIPS

(1) Peel and thinly slice the turnips.
(2) Cover them with boiling water and cook for 10 minutes.
(3) Melt the butter in a pan, then add the sugar and turnips.
(4) Stir and turn the turnips until they are golden brown, approximately 10 to 15 minutes (you may need to add more butter to keep them from burning).
(5) Season to taste with salt and pepper; serve.

❧ INGREDIENTS

4 medium-large turnips
2 tablespoons or more of butter
1 tablespoon of sugar
salt
pepper

SERVES 4

PEAS

(1) Put the peas in a pot and cover with boiling water.
(2) Add the salt, cover, and boil for approximately 15 minutes. Taste one or two peas after 7 minutes to check for doneness.
(3) Drain the peas and put them in a bowl.
(4) Add the butter and sugar.
(5) Season to taste with pepper; serve.

❦ INGREDIENTS

2 cups of peas
1 teaspoon of salt
4 tablespoons of butter
1 tablespoon of sugar
pepper

SERVES 4

MAYONNAISE OF CELERY

(1) Wash the celery and trim off the bottom of the bunch.
(2) Remove the strings from each stalk.
(3) Trim off the leaves.
(4) Cut each stalk horizontally into 3 equal parts.
(5) Combine the mayonnaise and rosemary.
(6) With a spatula, scoop a small amount of the mayonaise mixture into each celery trough.
(7) Arrange on a glass platter and garnish with rosemary leaves.

❦ INGREDIENTS

1 bunch of celery
1/3 cup of Homemade Mayonnaise (see page 61)
1 tablespoon of chopped fresh rosemary
1 sprig of fresh rosemary

SERVES 4–6

MINCEMEAT
(FOR MINCE PIE)

(1) Combine the beef, raisins, currants, brown sugar, molasses, orange and lemon juice and zest, citron, and spices in a large pot.

(2) Cook over a low heat for about an hour.

(3) Add the apples and cook until they are tender; let cool to room temperature.

(4) Add the suet, brandy, and wine.

(5) Let sit in the refrigerator for at least 3 days before using.

NOTE: *Many people are surprised to find that mincemeat really has meat in it. I know it sounds odd, and maybe a bit repellant, to make a dessert from top round—but believe me, this is absolutely the best recipe in the book. Please try it.*

NOTE: *Zest is just the outer part of the rind. Use a cheese grater to scrape off the colored part, but leave the white part.*

NOTE: *You can buy suet at a butcher shop.*

❦ INGREDIENTS

1/2 pound of top round beef, chopped fine
3/4 pound of raisins, minced
3/4 pound of currants
3/4 cup of brown sugar
1/4 cup of molasses
juice and zest from 1/2 an orange
juice and zest from 1/2 a lemon
1/8 pound of citron, minced
1 teaspoon of cinnamon, ground
1/4 teaspoon of cloves, ground
1/4 teaspoon of allspice, ground
1/4 teaspoon of ground mace
1/4 teaspoon of salt
3 cups of chopped apples
1/2 pound of beef suet, chopped fine
1/2 cup of brandy
1/4 cup of white wine

MAKES 2 9-INCH PIES

MINCE PIE

Preheat over to 425° F.

(1) Roll half of the dough out to fit a 9-inch pie plate with 1/2-inch overlap.
(2) Place the lower crust into the pie plate and trim the edges.
(3) Fill with mincemeat.
(4) Roll out the remaining dough.
(5) Moisten the edge of the lower crust with water.
(6) Cover the pie with the upper crust; trim and crimp the edges together.
(7) Use a fork to poke a few holes in the upper crust.
(8) Bake until the crust is golden, approximately 30–40 minutes. If crust starts to brown too quickly, place a sheet of tin foil over the top until it is done.

❦ INGREDIENTS

Old-Fashioned Pie Pastry (see page 86)
4 cups of Mincemeat (see page 74)

MAKES 1 9-INCH PIE

VANILLA ICE CREAM

(1) In the top of a double boiler, heat the milk to a gentle boil over water.
(2) Combine the egg yolks, sugar, and salt and beat until a light lemon color.
(3) Slowly add half of the hot milk, stirring constantly, then pour egg mixture into pot containing the milk.
(4) Add the vanilla bean and continue to cook until the mixture thickens slightly.
(5) Place custard in a bowl which is sitting in ice water to cool.
(6) Split the vanilla bean and scrape all the seeds out into the custard or add vanilla extract if not using the vanilla bean.
(7) Freeze according to the instructions of your ice cream freezer.
(8) Halfway through the freezing process, add the whipped cream. Finish freezing.

❦ INGREDIENTS

2 cups of milk
3 eggs, separated
1 cup of powdered sugar
a pinch of salt
1 vanilla bean or 1 tablespoon of vanilla extract
1 1/2 cups of heavy cream, whipped

NOTE: My 1894 cookbook lists a number of other flavors, including brown bread ice cream (make the vanilla recipe above, also add 1 cup of brown bread crumbs that have been toasted in the oven at the same time as the whipped cream), maraschino ice cream (the above vanilla with 1/4 cup of maraschino substituted for the vanilla), and nougat ice cream (the vanilla above, also add 1/2 cup of pistachio nuts, 1/2 cup of walnuts, and 1/4 cup of almonds, all chopped very fine, at the same time as the whipped cream).

SERVES 4

ANGEL FOOD CAKE

Preheat oven to 375° F.

(1) Sift the flour.
(2) Add the cream of tartar, then sift 5 more times.
(3) Sift the sugar.
(4) Beat the egg whites until they form stiff peaks.
(5) Gradually beat in the sugar.
(6) Gently fold in the flour, being sure to mix it thoroughly.
(7) Fold in the vanilla extract.
(8) Pour the batter into an ungreased angel food cake pan.
(9) Slice a knife through the butter to remove any air pockets.
(10) Bake for 30–35 minutes.
(11) Invert the pan on its stand or on a bottle.
(12) Cool completely before removing from baking pan.
(13) Dust with powdered sugar.
(14) Cut this cake with a serrated bread knife.

❦ INGREDIENTS

1 cup of flour
1 teaspoon of cream of tartar
1 1/2 cups of sugar
11 egg whites
1 teaspoon of vanilla extract (see note)
powdered sugar

NOTE: Be very careful when you separate the egg whites. If the tiniest bit of yolk gets in, the cake won't work.

NOTE: The simplest flavoring is vanilla. But you might want to substitute 1/2 a teaspoon of vanilla and 1/2 a teaspoon of almond extract or lemon juice.

NOTE: If you're used to angel food cake from a mix, this will not be anywhere near as fluffy. But that's the way it was then—and it's good.

SERVES 6–8

ENGLISH PLUM PUDDING

(1) Mix together the raisins, bread crumbs, flour, lemon zest, nutmeg, suet, candied orange peel, and brown sugar.

(2) Beat the eggs.

(3) Add the brandy to the eggs, and then add to the dry ingredients; mix well.

(4) Butter mold and fill no more than two-thirds full.

(5) Put on cover or cover with aluminum foil or wax paper held firmly in place with either string or rubber bands.

(6) Place the mold on a rack in a large pot.

(7) Add enough boiling water to come half way up the sides of the mold.

(8) Cover pot tightly and gently boil for 8 hours, adding water as it boils away. Pudding may be refrigerated at this point for several days.

(9) Remove from refrigerator and boil for 2 hours.

(10) Remove mold from the pot and set aside for 10 minutes.

(11) Unmold and set on a plate.

(12) Serve with Brandy Sauce (see page 82).

❦ INGREDIENTS

1/2 pound of raisins
6 ounces of stale bread crumbs
1/2 cup of flour
zest of 1/2 a lemon
1/2 a nutmeg, grated
1/2 pound of suet, chopped fine
1/4 pound of candied orange peel
1/3 cup of brown sugar
1/2 pound of currants
3 eggs
1/4 cup of brandy

NOTE: Brandy may also be poured over the pudding just before serving.

NOTE: Zest is just the outer part of the rind. Use a cheese grater to scrape off the yellow part, but leave the white part.

NOTE: You can buy suet at a butcher shop.

SERVES 8

CHARLOTTE RUSSE

Preheat oven to 375°F.

(1) Beat the egg yolks and sugar until thick and a pale lemon color.
(2) Mix in the lemon juice.
(3) Stir in the flour by hand, not with an electric mixer.
(4) Beat the egg whites until they form soft peaks.
(5) Gently fold egg whites into the batter.
(6) Pour the batter into a cake pan or mold which has been well oiled and dusted with powdered sugar.
(7) Bake for 30–35 minutes.
(8) Beat the egg whites until frothy.
(9) Beat in the sugar; continue beating until soft peaks form.
(10) Beat cream until frothy; then add flavoring.
(11) Beat cream until soft peaks form.
(12) Fold the whipped cream into the egg whites.
(13) Line a bowl or mold with the sponge cake.
(14) Spoon in the filling, being sure to remove any air pockets.

❦ INGREDIENTS

Sponge Cake:
10 eggs, separated
2 cups of sugar
1 teaspoon of lemon juice (flavoring)
2 cups of flour

Filling:
3 egg whites
3/4 cup of powdered sugar
1 cup of heavy cream
1/4 teaspoon of vanilla or lemon extract

NOTE: *Slice the sponge cake thin before lining the bowl with it. You want to leave room for as much filling as possible.*

NOTE: *Lady fingers can be substituted for the sponge cake. For flavoring, you could substitute orange extract or ground nutmeg.*

SERVES 6–10

GINGERBREAD

Preheat oven to 325° F.

(1) Whisk the butter until creamy.
(2) Beat in half the sugar.
(3) Beat egg with the rest of the sugar.
(4) Combine egg and butter mixtures.
(5) Sift dry ingredients together.
(6) Add dry ingredients to butter mixture.
(7) Add milk or hot water, and molasses.
(8) Beat until well mixed.
(9) Pour batter into a well greased bread pan.
(10) Bake for 35 minutes.

❧ INGREDIENTS

3 tablespoons of butter
1/2 cup of sugar
1 egg
1 1/2 cups of white flour
1 teaspoon of baking soda
1/8 teaspoon of salt
1 tablespoon of grated fresh ginger
1 teaspoon of cinnamon
1/2 cup of milk or hot water
1/2 cup of molasses

MAKES 1 LOAF

SUGAR PLUMS

(1) Put enough water to cover the plums into a pot. Add 1/2 cup of vinegar for every 3 quarts of water.
(2) Wash the plums and prick them all over with a fork.
(3) Place plums in the water and heat until plums start to float.
(4) Remove plums and set aside in a bowl.
(5) In a large pot, combine the sugar and the water.
(6) Bring the syrup to a boil, stirring constantly to dissolve the sugar.
(7) Pour sugar syrup over the plums.
(8) Let sit for 12–15 hours.
(9) Drain the syrup into a pot.
(10) Repeat from Step 6 four more times.
(11) Pull the remaining peel off the plums and arrange them on a pretty serving dish garnished with greens.

❦ INGREDIENTS

plums
vinegar
10 cups (5 pounds) of sugar
7 cups of water

NOTE: This recipe works best if the plums are not quite ripe yet.

BRANDY SAUCE

(1) Beat the egg yolks and whisk in the powdered sugar. Whisk until light.
(2) Beat the butter until creamy; then beat it into the egg yolk mixture.
(3) Slowly stir in a cup of boiling water, mixing each bit thoroughly, until the paste turns into a sauce. Once it does, you can add the remaining water more quickly. Stir over the heat until it thickens, then remove from the heat.
(4) Mix in the brandy.
(5) Pour the sauce over the plum pudding.

❦ INGREDIENTS

3 egg yolks
1/2 cup of powdered sugar
4 tablespoons of butter
1 cup of boiling water
2 tablespoons of brandy

MAKES ABOUT 1 CUP

ROSE JELLY

(1) Dissolve the gelatin in the cold water. Let it sit for 15 minutes.
(2) Add the boiling water and stir until the gelatin is dissolved.
(3) Add the sugar, orange juice, and orange zest. Boil for 1 minute.
(4) Pour mixture into a mold.
(5) Add some rose petals, or a whole rose blossom.
(6) Chill until firm.

❧ INGREDIENTS

1 1/2 ounces (6 packets) of unflavored gelatin
2 cups of cold water
4 cups of boiling water
1/2 cup of sugar
juice and zest of one orange

NOTE: Zest is just the outer part of the rind. Use a cheese grater to scrape off the orange part, but leave the white part.

NOTE: This dish as presented here is orange-flavored, but you could just as easily flavor it with lemon juice, apple juice, or anything else that will leave the gelatin clear.

SERVES 4-6

YULE DOLLIES

(1) Beat the butter and the sugar together until creamy.

(2) Add the eggs, cream, and vanilla extract; blend thoroughly.

(3) Combine flour and baking powder in a large mixing bowl.

(4) Make a large crater in the middle of the dry ingredients.

(5) Pour the wet ingredients into the crater (they will overflow it considerably), and stir with long, gentle strokes—as few as possible.

(6) When you can no longer stir, turn dough onto a lightly floured board and knead until dough is soft. Chill the dough in the refrigerator overnight.

Preheat oven to 350° F.

(7) Remove dough from the refrigerator and let it soften to room temperature.

(8) Roll dough out to 1/2-inch thick.

(9) Press out Yule Dollies with a cookie cutter that looks like a person.

❧ INGREDIENTS

1/4 pound of sweet butter
1 cup of sugar
2 eggs, lightly beaten
1/4 cup of heavy cream
1 teaspoon of vanilla extract
3 cups of flour
2 teaspoons of baking powder

(10) Arrange on a cookie sheet and bake for 17 minutes, or until slightly golden.

(11) Cool Yule Dollies on a wire rack, then ice and decorate them (see next page).

MAKES 4 YULE DOLLIES

ICING FOR YULE DOLLIES

(1) Beat the egg whites until they're frothy.
(2) Sift the sugar into a large bowl.
(3) Gradually beat sugar into the egg whites until the icing is very thick. (You may not need to use the entire pound of sugar.)
(4) Divide icing into batches, and tint each batch with a different food coloring.
(5) Cut the Yule Dollie's face from scrap (see note).
(6) Use a dot of icing to attach the face.
(7) Using a pastry bag, create colored-icing clothes. (If you're feeling expansive, Victorians also used beads and feathers to decorate Yule Dollies.)

❦ INGREDIENTS

1 pound of powdered sugar
2 egg whites
food coloring

NOTE: Scrap is any sort of Victorian graphic imagery. Upper class Victorian women with lots of time on their hands would cut out pictures that they liked and glue them into "scrap books." Nowadays, scrap is usually seen as that montage of Victorian images—children, adults, Santa Claus, winter scenes, Christmas trees, etc.—that you find on wrapping paper and shopping bags around the holiday season. Find an appropriate face or two for your Yule Dollies, then use a color photocopy machine to reproduce them in the right size. Peel the face off the Yule Dollie before you eat it.

OLD-FASHIONED PIE PASTRY

Preheat over to 425° F.

(1) Put the flour, baking powder, and salt into a bowl and mix it with a whisk.
(2) Cut the lard into the flour mixture with a pastry blender or 2 forks until the mixture resembles a coarse meal.
(3) Gradually add the milk, one tablespoon at a time, until the dough is just moist enough to form a ball.
(4) Divide the dough in half.
(5) Roll dough out on a floured board.
(6) Cut 1 tablespoon of butter into small bits and distribute over the surface of the dough.
(7) Fold both sides into the middle, turn 90° and fold into thirds again.
(8) Wrap the dough in wax paper and refrigerate for at least 20 minutes.
(9) Repeat from step 5 with second half of dough.

INGREDIENTS

2 cups of flour
2 teaspoons of baking powder
1/8 teaspoon of salt
1/4 pound of lard
1/2 cup of ice cold milk
2 tablespoons of butter

NOTE: This crust is not flaky. It seems more like a biscuit than a light pastry, but it's good—try it! If it's not what you want, substitute water for the milk.

MAKES 1 PIE

EGG NOG

(1) Separate the eggs.
(2) Beat the yolks in a bowl.
(3) Gradually add sugar; beat until pale yellow in color.
(4) Gradually beat in milk then cream.
(5) Stir in brandy and chill for several hours.
(6) Beat egg whites until they form stiff peaks.
(7) Fold egg whites into egg mixture.
(8) Pour into chilled glasses; sprinkle nutmeg on top.

❦ INGREDIENTS

2 eggs
2 tablespoons of sugar
2/3 cup of cream
2/3 cup of milk
2/3 cup of brandy
a pinch of freshly grated nutmeg

SERVES 4

ROMAN PUNCH

(1) Put the water, sugar, orange juice, and lemon juice in a pot. Stir over low heat until all of the sugar dissolves.
(2) Beat the egg whites into a stiff froth; then beat them into the punch.
(3) Freeze the mixture in an ice cream freezer until the mixture is very thick and cold, about 10-15 minutes.
(4) Just before serving, mix in the rum.

❦ INGREDIENTS

2 cups of water
2 cups of sugar
juice of 8 oranges
juice of 5 lemons
2 egg whites
2 tablespoons of Jamaican rum

SERVES 10–12

NOTES

RAW OYSTERS IN ICE BLOCK

"Perhaps no way are oysters so wholesome and delicious as from the shell, raw; and to have them in perfection, they should be very cold. A pretty and acceptable way to serve them is to take a large block of ice, make in it an excavation, in which set a glass dish, piling ice over its sides, and laying the oysters in the dish, sprinkling with pepper and salt and garnishing with sliced lemon."

WAFERS

"Wafers served with salads are the small salted wafers, of different kinds, and called by various names, such as the snowflake wafers, afternoon teas and the fleur-de-lis."

CELERY

"Wash and separate, laying aside the outer stalks and reserving only the [inner] blanched ones for present use. The others are very nice stewed or in soup, but are out of place for eating au naturel. Stand or lay the stalks in a celery glass or dish and place a few bits of cracked ice about them."

"Cut in thin slices across, put in a salad bowl with a wreath of leaves around the edge, a sprig in the middle, and salad dressing over the whole."

"A more ornamental way is to cut the stalks in pieces four inches long, split these four or five times with a sharp knife, lay in water till they curl, then remove to a glass dish; eat with vinegar, pepper and salt."

CHEESE

Cheeses typically served in winter months during the late Victorian period include American, Brie, Roquefort, Camembert, Stilton, Edam, and pineapple cheese.

Following the European style, a cheese course included bread to eat the cheese on (as we use crackers today). "The cheese may be served in a glass bowl, and handed round from right to left; or surrounded with the elegant serviette [napkin], and placed upon the cheese cloth. The bread may be served as usual, piled up on a crochet cloth in a plated bread-basket placed in the centre."

FRUIT

"Select a handsome dish. Put a table glass in the centre, cover with moss or leaves. Place a nice pine-apple on the top of the glass, and round it apples or pears with leaves between, then plums mingled with grapes. Much taste can be displayed in the arrangement of the fruit."

Grapes were usually white grapes (which we would think of as green). Other choices include oranges, bananas, figs, and dates. Raisins were so popular that some of the menus I've reprinted here give them their own listing.

NUTS

Nuts commonly served in December in the late 1800s include almonds (Jordan, paper shell, or princess varieties), walnuts, filberts (hazel nuts), pecans, and Brazil nuts. One magazine suggests a mix of filberts, almonds, and pecans; or of cracked hickory nuts, walnuts, and butternuts. A book from about the same period says, "Arrange them piled high in the centre of the dish; a few leaves around the edge of the dish will greatly improve the appearance."

OLIVES

"…the best and surest way for a housekeeper to have them perfect is to purchase the pitted olives in jars. You can find these at any first-class grocer."

CANDY

It's theoretically possible to make candy at home; but life is just too short. If you really want to make your own candy, get a book on it from the library and expect to spend a lot of time practicing— start in October, not on December 20. A better plan, though, might be to go to a fancy chocolate shop and buy some nice candies.

INDEX

Traditional Country Life Recipe Books from

BRICK TOWER PRESS

American Chef's Companion
Chocolate Companion
Fresh Herb Companion
Thanksgiving Cookery
Apple Companion

Forthcoming Titles

Clambake
Pumpkin Companion

MAIL ORDER AND GENERAL INFORMATION

Many of our titles are carried by your local book store or gift and museum shop. If they do not already carry our line please ask them to write us for information.

If you are unable to purchase our titles from your local shop, call or write to us.
Our titles are available through mail order. Just send us a check or money order for $9.95 per title with $1.00 postage to the address below or call us Monday through Friday, 9 AM to 5PM, EST. We accept Visa and Mastercard.

Send all mail order, book club, and special sales requests to the address below or call us. We would like to hear from you.

America Online: mckee@aol.com
Internet Bookstore: (ebooks-info@access.digex.net)
order number 12204 for the electronic edition
P12204 for the print edition

Brick Tower Press
1230 Park Avenue, 10th Floor
New York, NY 10128

Telephone & Facsimile
1-212-427-7139
1-800-68-BRICK